MW01247546

Scattered CHANGES

STEP LADDER CHANGES

OLLIE MARSHALL

Introduction

The book, *Scattered Changes* looks at the real world of events that have affected our lives. These events connect us as one, whether they may be local or global. They reaffirm us as members of the human race with many challenges that we must overcome. We must at times make very difficult decisions that may pound on us because it is a safe decision rather than the desired one. In making decisions that affect other lives, we should let the wisdom of our ancestors guide us. Ollie says let us meet and greet through the path of our ancestors. Let their string of hope reign within us. When we trod, let it be with their wisdom and understanding. Let their truth be grounded in our faith. Scattered lives consist of broken dreams that can abide in a new day when the feet follow the right path.

Events sometime determine how we interact with our surroundings. The author realizes it is impossible for us to be harmonious with our environment at times. A soldier cannot be at ease when he fights to stay alive within the war in Iraq. A person in a secured environment can experience emotional turmoil when others in that same surrounding pin thorns upon a path that make demands. Interpersonal relationship helps shape our lives, while the lack of a parent in a child's early years may send him on an infinite roller coaster ride. This roller coaster may conflict with all the good an individual has been exposed to at some point in life. Ollie explores the good and the bad of the essence of one's soul.

Scattered is the bit and pieces that tear at one's sanity. It is full of treasures and torn lives. It contains works that may bite the hand that places food in the mouth without a second thought.

She commences: *A tear moment may dry with a soft wind blow.*

But, in the end reality will take course whether it is harshly or gloriously.

She explores the harsh reality of growing old; she says: *The legs pointed in one direction sway in different directions. Each step cannot be maintained in a straight lane. Steps may be taken with a help of a cane. At some point the body may become yesterday's dream, while the mind may reflect upon three dimensions.*

Challenges are constantly placed upon us in this ever-changing society; therefore to maintain our sanity we must find a way to live with those demands. For Ollie, she has found her survival mold, the pen, as she says: Things will bounce upon you that can steal your soul.

> *Can you find a way out without a pout?*
> *What is your survival mold? Find it...*

Contents

I. **Unrest** 1

    A Mother Cries 3

    Fireball Nerves 4

    Katrina 5

    Refugees 6

    Dead 7

    Patterns 8

    Knees 9

    The Gambler 10

    The Hopeless Game 11

    Disillusion 12

    Looking 13

    Faison 14

    Amadou 15

II. **The Sun Wind Blows** 17

    Animals in Search 19

    Light 20

    Where Are You? 23

    Birds 27

    Beet 28

    Force 29

    Environmental 31

    Tsunami 33

    Winter 35

    Summer 36

    Air Soul 37

    The Farmer 38

    Drawn To Nature 39

III. Scattered **41**

    Lacking 43

    Downtrodden 44

    Rushing 45

    Scattered 46

    Infant 47

    Bare 48

    Struggle 49

    Too Soon 50

    Self-Conception 51

    Parents 52

    Dimensions 53

    Betrayal 54

    Nomad 55

    World of Fantasy 56

    Bones 57

    Lifeless 58

    Mate 59

    You 60

    Outsider 64

    Departure 67

    Sometimes 68

    Good-Bye, My Love 69

    Strangers in the Night 70

    Shame 71

    My Lover 72

    Tomorrow's Scars 73

    Good-Byes are harder than Hellos 74

    The Insanity 75

    Get Over It! 76

    Paula 77

    The Force 79

    An Act of Evil 80

    I Too Cry 81

Heart 82

Brown Eyed Girl 83

Interpretation...84

Venom...85

Truth 86

Weight...87

Ugly 88

Cocoon 89

The Will 90

Sacrifice...91

Temporary Insanity 92

IV. Existing...95

The Cobra...97

Passion...99

Newness 100

Passing...101

The Helper 102

Respect 103

Ancestors' Legacy 104

Moved 105

Survival Mold..106

Making It 107

Purity 108

Retirement 110

Unlock Your Door 111

Stumbling Forward 112

Stand or Not...113

"Flavia" 114

False Hope..115

The Blind Road 116

Rejuvenation 117

Changes..118

I

Unrest

A Mother Cries

Skeletons, tell facts of death, let there be none tomorrow.
This anguish shall cease to exist, the day you are put to rest.
You have stolen his cries of pain with the joy we shared.
There is no laughter in my house.

Skeletons, tell facts of death, let there be none tomorrow.
The streets are painted with the shadow of death.
The laughter and cries of tomorrow I will hear no more.
The transition child growth I will see no more.

Skeletons, tell facts of death, let there be none tomorrow.
Down the street, yesterday I heard the cry.
When neighbors came calling today, children were chained.
Yesterday's smile, tomorrow's hope will be heard
in another, not the voice I yearn to hear.

Skeletons, tell facts of death, let there be none tomorrow.
A dreadful destroyer continues to deprive
a generation of tomorrow.
Shall it remain an unknown phenomenon,
striking only black males?
Five went walking to disappear without a
trace, guesses leave no answers.

Skeletons, tell facts of death, let there be none tomorrow.
An accident today, tomorrow a life will be taken.
An Atlanta's mother cries, a community is being held hostage.
Skeletons, tell facts of death, let there be none tomorrow.

Fireball Nerves

The nerves were fireballs pounded on aches.

Memories of time, times of memories,
everything moved on, none, stopped.

Emotions, anxiety, sleeplessness, night and day became one.

The nerves were fireballs pounded on aches.

The jungle panic attract was on me.

The door splintered my smallest finger.

The nerves were fireballs on aches.

The rapid heartbeats came steadily.

The full bed lay empty, nothing touches.

The nerves were fireballs pounded on aches.

Katrina

Silence spoke death.
Children had pale faces reaping signs of hunger.
Mothers' faces held silent tears.
A mill smell full with feces filled the air.

Silence spoke death.
When thirst went, life dwindled.
The bodily pain and hunger existed with life.
Eyes wide opened with closed canned pulse.

Silence spoke death.
Seeking dry bread and water to consume, toddlers moved aimlessly.
Shoes laced not, families paced and waited to be rescued.
Death's rattle came and went.

Silence spoke death.
Leaders walked without shame.
Who will take the blame, America is not a third world country?
Poor folk are dying with the greatest resources.

Refugees

They called them refugees.
How can one be a refugee in his country?
They sought safety within their borders.
Could it be a country that prides itself on democracy?

They called them refugees.
They had no food in the midst of a flood.
They were dehydrated, and rated unworthy.
No one came to their need, so they went looking.

They called them refugees.
Survival it was, but they called them looters.
Many found food by the pound to try to meet those in need.
They sought to be rescued, but no one brought the resources.

They called them refugees.
People wanted shelter safety, not separation like slavery.
It was a flood disaster, not a political or religious war.
Was it simply a persecution of class and color when the end came?

Dead

Bodies floated about my window.
Was it real, or just a dream?
Yesterday, I was a zombie.
How did I survive?

Bodies floated about my window.
Unable to see land, the stench of flesh surrounded me.
Trees floated like sponges.
A mother and her infant, floated by, connected as one.

Bodies floated about my window.
Lifeless dehydrated bodies lay in corners.
The Super Dome should have been the net of safety.
People cried and died of hunger; faces of death surrounded me.

Bodies floated about my window.
They packed us in without food and water,
days passed, and I wondered…
Why were we there?
To leave this ravaged place, we stepped over bodies.

Patterns

Behavior patterns—let--it not be fixed upon me.
A ritual will detail lifestyle with every act.
When duty speaks, we will meet and greet warmly.
When mud swallows, our neighbors extend a reaching hand.

Behavior patterns—let--it not be fixed upon me.
Talk and walk with a smile, reach the human
soul without the thought of you.
Let not your face break let not the soul.
Let it console the spirit of others.

Behavior patterns—let--it not be fixed upon me.
If you feel a tear let it come without the ceremony.
Let your life honor others without your fancy coat.
Teach and reach for the stars with those who have no song.

Behavior patterns—let--it not be fixed upon me.
Touch my hand and come when I have not worldly possession?
Read my eyes, come to me, feel the broken heart.
Cry with me and not for me; then we can
change ugliness into beauty.

Knees

The legs pointed sway in different directions.
The ligaments are torn with deep pain.
The veins are separated in rows.
The aches are deep with a squeaking cry.

The legs pointed sway in different directions.
Each step cannot be maintained in a lane
that must be taken with a cane.
Years have rendered its tow: strength has slowly dissipated.
The mind moves rapidly, the body becomes yesterday's dream.

The legs pointed sway in different directions.
The hands curve fully with an uncontrolled nerve.
Today and yesterday's generation connection becomes clearer.
Today is a stiff reality, a day without the bounce.

The legs pointed sway in different directions.
The swelling enlarged muscles, exhibit no mercy.
The aches elevate upward, leaving an unbearable headache.
The echoed prayer, Father, will you cease this
awesome pain that ravages this body?

The Gambler

The gambler is in a ramble.
Mood searcher, head covered in a hood.
Edge dancer, the dance never ends.
Body twisted in knots.

The gambler is in a ramble.
Preamble the mind, disable the body.
Light in the day has creaked into one long night.
Each coin becomes the next denomination.

The gambler is in a ramble.
Every jackpot becomes the progressive one.
Money chaser bounces from one machine to the next.
A bit confused, dazed, the big hit looker.

The gambler is in a ramble.
Will you free me surrounded within this the
atmosphere, betting in the moment?
Risk taker, bristle the floor, none conceivable
stop, looking to top the house.
Body drained, looking to escape until the next time, it never ends.

The Hopeless Game

The dangling coins are outdated.
The machines now have flinching lights.
A man began to express joy as a boy.
The heart starts to beat.

The dangling coins are outdated.
The paper carries the weight.
A billion or trillion is not enough for the habit.
A penny is a bit too much for the feed.

The dangling coins are outdated.
A new world has claimed the mind.
It is in a total bind, out of control.
The bills have become secondary to none.

The dangling coins are outdated.
The mortgage, the taxes, and insurance go unpaid.
The phone rings without a pick up.
It is a pillow bounce about without a cushion...
The dangling coins are outdated.
It calls and malls a hopeless mind.

Disillusion

It is disillusion with a form of reality intact.
Facts a stretched reality with fancy, whipped in the core.
One world has come with two different shoes' perspectives.
Convenience ached in one, while the other
is a hidden ton of deception.

It is disillusion with a form of reality intact.
Innocent escaped stories that are retold.
The storyteller retells the story as listeners come forth.
It is an act to recreate a fact to put oneself in the light.

It is disillusion with a form of reality intact.
Dance with me and I will lance you with my
aroma; it's the best of all the rest.
Let us take you to lunch; there will be no punch on
the table, just a bunch of us trying to free ourselves
from this bondage that encages our minds.
We will breathe together, peeling each
moment that cement us into oneness.

It is disillusion with a form of reality intact.
The conscious displays conflict with inner-self.
The non-conscious stays in a state of numbness.
The two details one's life.

Looking

This crave lost mind is on a no pave street searching endlessly.
Credit card maxed, plus one check.
Reality crushed into a mush.
Picture a mouse loose in a city.

This crave lost mind is on a no pave street searching endlessly.
It's a mind looking for footsteps to walk on air.
Reality has escaped; the head holds only sound of clicking coins.

Each coin crashes into the next, until there is none.

This crave lost mind is on a no pave street searching endlessly.
Faces stripped bare, tell stories.
Smiles are miles unseen.
Hopes, disappear when pockets are bleached cleaned.

This crave lost mind is on a no pave street searching endlessly.
Each day says, not again, until the next time.
Today's play is sought to erase yesterday's unlucky day.
It's a game that has no ending.

Faison

Who stopped Brain, prior to Faison?
City fathers protected his unlawful acts.
He respected none; they did not care.
He doped the symbol people hold dear and near.

Who stopped Brain, prior to Faison?
They pinned him for bodies in rows that lie in graves.
He carved lives, like the butcher carves meat.
City fathers danced with release, debated not.

Who stopped Brain, prior to Faison?
His feet stomped faces like walking on grass.
It was a boxed grave, formality followed.
His high was in full force.

Who stopped Brain, prior to Faison?
They closed their eyes and did not see.
They closed their ears and did not hear.
Will they now know, Faison's death laid on their steps?

Amadou

Forty-one bullets, at twenty-two, they took his life.
Yesterday they sang the song of hatred between you and me.
We are connected; yesterday, they sang the
song of hatred between you and me.
But, why does it always have to be signed in blood!
We ran from each other, elevating that
falsehood of sisters and brothers.

Forty-one bullets, at twenty-two, they took his life.
Excuses cannot explain away his death, not with forty-one bullets.
Will people care enough not to let another life go this way?
Must some people always pay with a life, just because
their skin processes the color of bronze?

Forty-one bullets, at twenty-two, they took his life.
A rich life has been taken, be it a native African, a Haitian or
an African-American, skin color has placed us into one.
Invisible color, we move as one.
Roots we share, though many have sought to
destroy, skin brings us into a reality.

Forty-one bullets, at twenty-two, they took his life.
What will we do to eliminate this growing tragedy?
Will we stand and hold hands?
Will we stand amiss, while returning to days gone?

II

The Sun
Wind Blows

Animals in Search

It was a dish that held a motionless fish.
The stink filled the ocean shore.
The remains city pelicans lumbered in their track.
The shore line was lined with debris of pelicans.

The hummingbirds hovered over once garden flowers bed.
Only stems remained where flowers once flourished.
Sparrows searched for seeds to crush.
The heat had consumed the seeds leaving everything bare.

Giraffes and zebras went searching for plants.
The atmosphere was none inviting.
The fog and smog filled the eyes.
The animals cried out for release.

Technology brought a costly temporary convenience.
Luscious cars have shortened the time between two points.
The pleasure of convenience has had it cost to paid.
Will we take progress and move cautiously in the future.

Light

This morning I awaken in light.
The darkness of yester morning was gone.
The moment I reflected on you, light blazed in my mist.
When I walk not with thee, your mercy holds and carries me.
Let me not forget, the light I hold today,
is my reward pay from you.

This morning I awaken in light.
When the stone of licks have hit my back, you have picked me up.
When I have fallen, you have lifted me into your light.
You have taught me how to walk by faith
when darkness surrounds me.

This morning I awaken in light.
To see your greatness with your blessings you have stored upon me.
Your mercy has always been with me
even when it was not deserved.
Like the sight of a flight coming to rest,
your goodness flows within me.

This morning I awaken in light.
Your salvation's gift has given me peace.
Peace to move forward, to leave unpleasant
thoughts upon your shoulders.
It is this gift that allows my heart to be
blessed in your name Father.

WHERE ARE YOU?

Where is My Flush?

These waves are merciless.
They have galloped my soul.
My flush is no more.

The dawn of life surrounds me.

Birds

It is the bird that I long to hear to bring near.
Its beak is short and thick.
It crushes seeds as one brushes teeth.
Could it be an eye of a sparrow?

It is the bird that I long to hear to bring near.
Its beak is long and thin.
It dips deep into the flower and nips out the food.
Could it be the hummingbird that long to hear?

It is the bird that I long to hear to bring near.
Its body is nourished from its hooked beak.
It is the symbol that carries my county.
Could it be the vulture or an eagle that represents me?

It is the bird that I long to hear to bring near,
Its hard beak chips the wood in search of food.
The trees carry its meal deep beneath the bark.
Could it be the woodpecker that searches the forest?

Beet

The world goes beat, beat, beat, beat and beat.

The leafy goes crunch, crunch, crunch, crunch above my feet.

This frame of life carries me without a
taste of sweet, just, bare and raw.

You are the stone leafy, cooking and crunching me.

Yet, I am still standing, pilling and wondering how.

Force

Hold on to old memories that shine within you.
Noise stares outside that has put you into panic mode.
The wind roars.
Sandy is in control, individuals respected not.

Hold on to old memories that shine within you.
Materials are river gone, debris floats.
The streets have disappeared, river gone.
Someone is purged from the flowing river.

Hold on to old memories that shine within you.
Memories found only in the mind.
Collected memories float now in the river.
Silence met silence, empty faces, lines of tears rolled.

Hold on to old memories that shine within you.
Lips come with stories full.
Sandy was the bull that ran with full force.
The eyes sore viewed the unidentifiable rubbish.

ENVIRONMENTAL

Life Storms of Life

Tsunami

Three fourth minus one came to claim another portion.
Community towns disappeared.
What blame do I have?
The ocean water went beyond the shore.

Three fourth minus one came to claim another portion.
The huge waves crashed upon the shore.
What blame do I have?
An earthquake created the giant wave.

Three fourth minus one came to claim another portion.
The breaker wave had no mercy that day.
What blame do I have?
The souls of many went beyond eye sight.

Three fourth minus one came to claim another portion.
Surfers succumbed to the wind wave that day.
What blame do I have?
When the earth speaks, do I not hear?

WINTER

Summer

Life is bursting forth through spring conception.
Toddlers continue to have the run of the fun as new birth comes.
The sheep watches over the lamb with
a beep to keep the prey away.
The bark will keep away any prey that comes near her puppies.

Life is bursting forth through spring conception.
The kittens are purring while muffing in the fresh air.
The kids and lambs are sharing the meadow
that stand high in green.
The cubs are playful where mother bear scouts
for food in the field that stands bare.

Life is bursting forth through spring conception.
The cow grazes and the calf yet wonders about the new world.
Will it be one of shelter or doom?

Life is bursting forth through spring conception.
The pig lies still nursing its piglets while the chicks dig holes as
they peck into the ground chipping away at discarded food.
Who will nurse the unwanted infant that came
into the world without a thought this day?
Will it be hidden in a purse until life breathes no more?

Air Soul

What are you without those who have
crossed the past you have walked?
Are you a blank table; or a balloon filled with air?
Are you a house filled with things that connect with nothing?
Are you thankful for the gratitude others
have bestowed upon you, my sister?

What are you without those who have
crossed the past you have walked?
Are you a broken chain without links to
connect that train that carry the whole?
Are you the one who cries in silence because
the biological string doesn't connect?
Are you thankful for the gratitude others have
bestowed upon you, my brother?

What are you without those who have
crossed the past you have walked?
Are you a store without the storekeeper?
Are you without worth who has been beaten into a pulp?
Are you thankful for the gratitude others have bestowed upon you?

What are you without those who have
crossed the past you have walked?
Are you the one who claims to be an island
because there is a lack of caring?
Are you broken-hearted because another was chosen over you?
Are you thankful for the gratitude others have bestowed upon you?
Or your eyes closed because you cannot see beyond you?

The Farmer

The corn stalk is complete with its fullness.
The crop will be shortly harvested.
Mouths are waiting in the wing to be filled.
The farmer is gathering the crew.

The green bean vines have overlapped.
The outer shells are bursting loose.
They are waiting to be harvested, and the machines are down.
The farmer searches for hands to pull in the crop.

He searches the beach to harvest the peach orchard.
Working hands sit not at the beach, rough hands are far beyond.
The sun beams hot on the body.
To pick and carry the fruit out, there are
orchard line rows to be filled.
The farmer stands in the mist, wondering
will he be able to feed the hungry.
It is through him, we eat to breathe.
The farmer stands helplessly seeking a crew to gather his crop.
Each day we eat fully, not wondering how we eat to breathe.

Drawn To Nature

Come sense with me.
Juices are netted in fruits.
Rattle snakes are curved to strike at their prey.
Come sense with me.

Come sense with me.
Sugar canes wait to be harvested for their sweetness.
Wooded trees are lined up like clustered of rice.
Come sense with me.

Come sense with me.
The cows are grazing in the pasture.
The lambs are baaing all about.
Come sense with me.

Come sense with me.
Horses are quenching their thirst at the pond.
Rabbits are skipping and hopping all about.
Come sense with me.

Come sense with me.
The frogs are jumping and drumming in the water.
The rocky gravel roads are foot messaging.
Come sense with me.

Come sense with me.
The clouds are fluttering all about, floating endlessly.
The wind comes with a breath of fresh air.
Come sense with me.

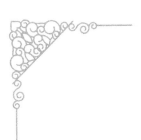

III

Scattered

Lacking

Courage came to my door, and I had not let it enter.
It came back and I stood behind the door and wished it away.
When it came again, my breath I held, hoping it to leave.
When the knock stopped, I wondered why
courage sought me this day.

Courage came to my door, and I had not let it enter.
My mind held fear that lacked a deep sense of bravery.
With chains they forced the door open, and
then the closet became my locked door.
The difficulty to rescue me stood not in others but me.

Courage came to my door, and I had not let it enter.
Love had come once, but never again, because
fear had closed the broken heart.
The sunshine was bright with great light, yet
one small cloud shunned the sight of it.
With eyes opened wide I could not see, my
mind held the key that unlocked the sun.

Courage came to my door, and I had not let it enter.
The life of love is bottomed up because I have
moved into a state of emptiness.
Never lose the will to love; that is the loss of
self, with courage comes strength.
Courage came again and again, but I was
locked up in yesterday's past.

Downtrodden

A homeless drifter, lost in self, wandering aimlessly.
A corner that houses those discarded as trash?
Debris doomed for land field holds human remains.
The heart beats in the heat and cries at the sight of night.

A homeless drifter, lost in self, wandering aimlessly.
A lost soul is somewhere in the midst of a crowded street.
Survival answers are sought but none hold to the test.
Dungeon blinded, one searches and reaches for the light.

A homeless drifter, lost in self, wandering aimlessly.
An echo of affirmation is sought, none to be found.
A powerless and unprotected female still stands tall.
Society puts its feet upon her head and labels her as a mad woman.

A homeless drifter, lost in self, wandering aimlessly.
The insanity of a woman, seeks only a place to call her own arena.
Society refuses to acknowledge her individuality.
She cries in the darkness of night and prays daylight never comes.

Rushing

Let not this day bind into empty space.
Net it into your consciousness.
Your presence sees tomorrow, but your
consciousness erases this day.
Crushing and rushing this moment will not grasp the unknown.

Let not this day bind into empty space.
Let this moment live through those who wish to touch.
Perceive what may never come.
Touch those who stand before the eyes.

Let not this day bind into empty space.
A child that touches today may model your steps.
Let the bell carry your thoughts well.
Put the best into your nest; take time to
see the birds without wings.

Let not this day bind into empty space.
Rush not, the small things may crush.
Take time to exhale, let the air breathe in, and give life.
Live the present, combined with the past and the future.

Scattered

Scattered lives, scattered treasures,
scattered lies, scattered on me.

Infant

Your mind tosses back and forth as an infant.
Can you not pave a permanent way for a new wave to come?
The sound of your voice is ever unassuming.
Your lock on the door has seldom opened to the knock.

Your mind tosses back and forth as an infant.
You never shine in a straight line to create definite light.
Your marbles are sometimes as loose as the moose in Alaska.
Without a second try, you cry and proceed to relinquish your goal.

Your mind tosses back and forth as an infant.
You come home to seek answers when the wind blows the plow.
Your search is to find oneself, and reach the goal of inner beauty.
Like cracker jacks in the box, you are looking
for the prize when you are the prize.

Your mind tosses back and forth as an infant.
You change as seasonal flowers, burst balloons, just
to seek, search, what is anew and unseen.
You are the rose; there is not a need to look for one.
Look inside; exhale the beauty and strength
that has already carried you.

Bare

After you, I was left bare.
The laughter I once shared with you now escapes me.
I once smiled to see the beauty in you.
I once laughed to see the glare in your eyes.

I once moved within your time zone.
I once glorified your independence.
I once saw your profound strength.
I once saw what dawned anew in you without me.

I once danced--gladly to your steps.
I once saw your beautiful smile.
I once experienced your dark days.
I once shared your thoughts.

I once felt your silent words, words that went unspoken.
I once felt your patience.
I once felt the pain that labored in your body.
I once rejoiced to feel your joy but now you are gone and
I am bare.

Struggle

Both, black and white are often within the line of gray.

One day this can become a dichotomy struggle.

The classifier determines its status.

The terms are elevated only by the perceiver.

Ownership gained forcedly is elevated;

While another struggles to maintain a sense of balance.

The continued struggle with oneself begins without an end.

Too Soon

Did I give up too soon when midnight parks felt my step no more?
Did I give up too soon when the dim light
disappeared over the horizon?
Did I give up too soon when college funds
went without a student in class?
Did I give up too soon when our path
crossed without a spoken word?

Did I give up too soon when anchored,
desperately to believe in you?
Did I give up too soon when I was relieved just to see your face?
Did I give up too soon when the road to respect was no more?
Did I give up too soon when your progress was less than a toad?

Did I give up too soon when the truth never
seemed to be a part of your vocabulary?
Did I give up too soon when my body
became too weak to move forward?
Did I give up to soon when my thoughts
of you put me in the hospital?
Did I give up too soon when your best existed only in my mind?

Did I give up too soon when your behavior rattled my nerves?
Did I give up too soon when my legs were
too weak to move forward?
Did I give up too soon when I battled for my survival over you?
Did I give up too soon when your lies became your truth?

Self-Conception

The time has been too short, yet too long.
Your mood has crept into its own world.
The beep of a baby sounds no more.
You have come of age, freedom to be free.

The time has been too short, yet too long.
You have a world of your own.
You bite in the night with your secrets.
You cry in the day to receive pay for work undone.

The time has been too short, yet too long.
Footsteps creep deep in the night.
Your steps with truth will never portray this land.
Your walk and talk itch through your eyes.

The time has been too short, yet too long.
Wisdom comes through experiences, not an open door.
With your conception, your imaginary games must have names.
Could this world have damaged you so
deeply, that love has escaped?

Parents

What have I done?
I know I do not see it clearly.
Did I give you to the wolves or did I
open the door for you to grow?
It was three rows to follow, but you selected not one.
Will you spread your wings?
Will you crawl into a cave to let it swallow you?
I cannot thread your life's needle.
This is the last straw.
You must put away the waste to create a quality life.
Will one come to my door to say you are no more?
This I do not know, but there are no
more tears to pour in the river.
What will I do or what should I do if this day shall come to past?
Will I echo the many conversations that we have had to embrace?
This is a race I do not wish to explore.
Will I feel guilt that you are no longer in eyesight?
Perhaps my feet will take me into your light;
That will be pleasing to my sight.
Will I wear guilt over my face or hide it within my body?
This is an avenue that cannot truly be explored now.
There is everywhere a wide range of emotions displayed.
Will I miss you and seek you out, to know where you walk?
It is an issue that talk will not resolve;
You will always be dear in my heart.
Your drum will beat near and far wherever I anchor.
Will the day come when the wind blows your name?
If so, let me reflect upon those thoughts of the past.
Reality will put everything into perspective.
But will I be able to cope?

Dimensions

You are one with many dimensions.
Will you please let me be today?
Ricky Prick, will you please stop kicking my meat?
The children are crying in the dark, you are the father.

You are one with many dimensions.
Your fist pounds with sounds in their ears.
Helplessly, they cry silently, Stop…! Stop…! Stop…!
Their little bodies curved openly into halls wrapped like balls.

You are one with many dimensions.
Your actions today will intertwine with their tomorrows.
Their legacy will be rooted through you.
Why have your children looked upon their ancestors with frowns?

You are one with many dimensions.
You pound my head into the ground.
My eyes are swollen and you see not the agony laced in their faces.
You hear your only cry.

You are one with many dimensions.
You hold the stage of rage upon your shoulders.
Society bites you, you hit and ditch me.
Are you determined to destroy the mother's image of love?

You are one with many dimensions.
Let not your sons duplicate the same pill
into the root of the community.

Betrayal

What have you done my brother?

This is a line fence of betrayal.

It stands before my eyes, but I don't want to see.

What have you done my brother?

Money should not replace morals.

Oh, my brother, what have you done!

It is not I you sell, but a people.

It is a wedge driver, another unneeded dimension.

One Texan dragged, chained, lifeless still body,
forty-one bullets, in another, unthinkable!

But my brother, me, sold how could that be?

How could I be sold my brother?

Today's eyes are more skeptical than yesterday's.

The millennium is here…mind plantation supersedes bondage.

Oh, my brother, what have you done!

What…have…you…done…?

Nomad

A tearful moment that recaps yesterday's regrets.
Weep not; cry your future, not the past.
Your face speaks the deeds gone.
This moment, the tears run, that will dawn with the sun.

A tearful moment will dry with a soft wind blow.
What do I do with these few pennies?
I wish your independence.
Reality must speak, not a wish bottled in an unreal Jenny's dish.

A tearful moment that recaps yesterday's regrets.
One repeats mistakes with regrets that should
not be, a duplicated hopeless circle…
An uncanny goal of hope has taken over
the mind like dope in the body.
Hope dances on the land of mercy, yet walks into repeated fire.

A tearful moment that recaps yesterday's regrets.
Where is the learned lesson? Is there one to emulate here?
We cry with dry or river tears but tread in the same muddy ditch.
Where is the lesson to be learned here?

World of Fantasy

My hope died the day you married.
I picked up my shoes, laced them and walked.
Miles separated us, but the thoughts of you remained.
I tossed here and there, but your face
anchored deeply into my thoughts.

My hope died the day you married.
I wondered when the ache would go.
But, it had already caged into a stone.
Miles of smiles I sought, but none came upon me.

My hope died the day you married.
Endless mornings blended into nights.
The lights of day became shadows of nights.
There were no meds to cure this wound.

My hope died the day you married.
One step each day had to be taken, moving forwardly.
If memory serves me right, you never existed.
It was only a fantasy created that I had to rid myself.

Bones

My world is out of order.
My flesh feels like dry bones.
My mind feels like it is at the end.
Lord, will you help me to come alive?

My world is out of order.
Lord, will you help me to put things into perspective?
Let the joy of you come upon me.
Lord, will you touch these dry bones?

My world is out of order.
Will you give me insight so I can see light in others?
Will you help me to bring joy to others?
Lord, will you cleanse my heart so I can feel the warmth of others?

My world is out of order.
Lord, let the joy of sunshine be within me today.
Lord, will you lift me up beyond my spirit?
Lord, will you let the spirit of your joy surround me this day?

Lifeless

There you are, at my steps, looking at me!

What are you going to take this time?

You first took my heart without stopping for a beat.

You came back and took my mind.

You left me in a complete worthless bind.

If that was not enough, you kept on nibbling.

You took my nose, toes, not only boxed
them, but caged them in a hole.

You took not the time to prop me against the wall.

You throw me on the ground with pin pegs sticking in my legs.

I see, I hear, I have no sufficient meaning.

You poke iron in my eyes, I cannot feel or see.

Body parts remain saddled into dirt, walk on me, it real.

What are you?

Mate

They went searching for a mate.
Will it become a date of reality?
Will they catch your society's trophy?
Will forbidden fruit come together?

They went searching for a mate.
Many elected not to walk the runway.
Will the free spirits walk and talk as one?
Let them meet and greet as one.

They went searching for a mate.
Creamed corn and nappy hair sought to be one.
Will they embrace their power to create a new world?
Will their self-outweigh their family roots?

They went searching for a mate.
Beauty defines family roots.
Beauty came both with nappy hair laced with
beads, sky blue eyes and straight hair.
Will pride walk with each without losing self?

You

Your mind has ripped my soul bare.
The thought of your lips pressed gently
against mines is a blessed hope.
The aches of my nerves cry out for you, you alone.
The touch of your hands pressed against
my body cries out for more.

Your mind has ripped my soul bare.
Your smile has reached beyond a mile to
touch the thoughts of mines.
Your skin blended in my bowl and I felt
the spoon deep within my gravy.
The gravy gushed over the pot, in that
moment, the hot fire rested peacefully.

Your mind has ripped my soul bare.
The cold air came and you pulled me into the warmth.
In the space of that warmth, I surrendered it all to you.
You caressed me and pressed my dreams into reality.

Your mind has ripped my soul bare.
The floor was cracked and the door was closed,
just for me, you created a new path.
I came to dance a new song just for you.
But when I opened my eyes, it was just a dream.
Sadly, I stumbled and stumbled, wanting to return to that dream.

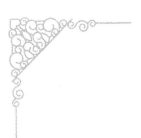

OUTSIDER

Outsider

Are you an outsider within this family atmosphere?
This is a family of oneness.
Two stand as one and one stands as all.
Solidarity of oneness is none other than one.

Are you an outsider within this family atmosphere?
You are two cultures, yet the same mingling into one.
You are trying to mingle to understand one another.
Distance, two roads traveled and intersected into one.

Are you an outsider within this family atmosphere?
It is a history that has touched each soul.
It is the line of color that has sought out you both.
There are roads to travel but two must meet to understand.

Are you an outsider within this family atmosphere?
Will an outsider ever merge into this
particular family value system?
Hands are stressed on line to embrace the thoughts others hold.
Yet, first there are so many thoughts that need to be untangled.

DEPARTURE

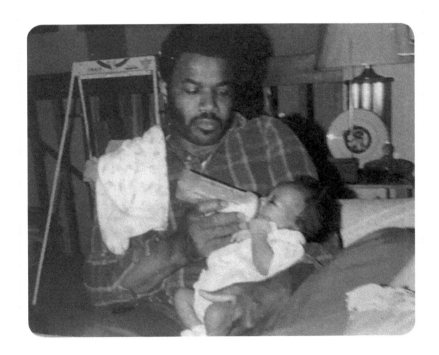

Sometimes

Sometimes tearless they cry.

Sometimes they die while still walking among the living.

Sometimes they make breathless sounds.

Sometimes they shout without others hearing.

Sometimes bedded in rocks they move in air.

Sometimes they laugh.

Sometimes invisible they gather in crowds.

Sometimes burdens overload their barrels.

Sometimes they stand motionless.

Sometimes their gestures unravel their past
without one vast spoken word.

Sometimes they move with pain, the
doctors cannot locate in the vein.

Sometimes their colorful thoughts die on the stage.

Sometimes they must create a new beginning.

Good-Bye, My Love

It is time to say good-bye, my love.
The hatred that stands in my heart cannot be.
Let your thoughts be pure and go with my love.
There are no friends to bid farewell.

It is time to say good-bye, my love.
The cord must be broken, the ending chapter closed.
To have endured the pain of anxiety tells the untold story.
A human soul, a family is priceless; one cannot
compare the pain of one's lost.

It is time to say good-bye, my love.
One loves and gives through his soul.
One plans and moves quickly through objectivity.
The final chapel ends, the prepared winner celebrates victory.

It is time to say good-bye, my love.
Dreams vanish and disappear as friends and foes in family.
The bare essence of truth lies in the heart.
If the truth has been portrayed, stand high and celebrate.

It is time to say good-bye, my love.
You gave me both lies and dreams.
Perhaps the day will come for me to understand the "why",
now let me wonder not, the thought too painful.
You have confused me with your face and back.

It is time to say good-bye, my love.
The bitterness, sadness should not be.
Time should have stopped with that hot summer romance.
Innocence was stolen, but growth took place.

Strangers in the Night

Come; come love one, strangers, in the night treading not.

Come; come love me, strangers, in the night treading not.

Come; come tickle my fancy, strangers, in the night treading not.

Come; come tickle my fancy, strangers, in the night treading not.

Come; come weary soul, strangers, in the night treading not.

Come; come weary soul, strangers, in the night treading not.

Come; come ride the Nile; strangers, in the night treading not.

Come, come ride the Nile; strangers, in the night treading not.

Shame

Shame has come and gone.

There is no need for good-byes.

Shame has come and gone.

The time to move has elapsed.

Shame has come and gone.

Shoes are laced, tremble not.

Shame has come and gone.

Hands misplaced will be no more.

Shame has come and gone.

You have dishonored another without a cause.

Shame has come and gone.

There is a need for good-byes.

My Lover

You have been the chosen one.
How did you treat me today?
Did you caress me or call to say "I'm sorry?
I won't be over."

Will you meet my need tomorrow?
Will there be a telephone call?
Will you say "I had to leave town?"
Will the emergency be for one day or a week?

Maybe tomorrow will be the time of love-making.
I will not have to wonder your where about…
Your lips will fill mine with kisses.
Your body will turn to each given task.

Will there be an image sitting by the window to receive another?
Will I be waiting patiently for the sound of a telephone?
Will your body stand by me?
Will your mind and soul never leave for another?

Tomorrow's Scars

Give me not your soul.

What was done cannot be undone.

Give me not your tears.

What was done cannot be undone.

Give me not your pity.

What was done cannot be undone.

Give me not sorrow and grief.

What was done cannot be undone.

Give me not your apology.

What was done cannot be undone.

Give me not guilt.

What was done cannot be undone.

Give me not your somber face.

What was done cannot be undone.

Give me not your remorse.

What was done cannot be undone.

Give me nothing, go and enjoy the priceless gift.

What was done cannot be undone.

Good-Byes are harder than Hellos

Good-byes are harder than hellos.
This occasion has been drawn with sadness.
Chained memories have gone through seasons.
Character diversities are challenged,
impossible at times to leave behind.

Good-byes are harder than hellos.
When winter comes and goes, the wound will be fresh and cold.
It will plug the heart center, chilling pain running down the spine.
Reality begins to take its course with the touch of spring.

Good-byes are harder than hellos.
The hot humid summer creates a desire to
escape with complex thoughts.
It is an unbalanced treadmill reflecting upon
the past, the present, and the future.
The will to move on begins to pound harder and harder.

Good-byes are harder than hellos.
The, autumn comes, the leaves and a new day has dawned.
The pain of growth has taken its course;
it is time for friends to greet.
A new day has dawned.

The Insanity

We try to structure sanity, out of insanity.

We pollute the body, seeking solutions.

Days locked into nights, rip tides pounding the shores.

Locked into a dungeon, the soul unable to escape fireballs,

We try to structure sanity, out of insanity.

Get Over It!

Hey, get over it!
Time has elapsed, years have merged.
Let the element of reality take place.
Take the dream out of your fantasy.

Hey, get over it!
Reality has always been upon you.
Open your eyes to breathe realness, surrounded by facts.
What you perceived never existed.

Hey, get over it!
Your life's quality is incomplete over a fantasy.
Will eyes tell your agenda, with your book wide open?
Self crying out; enough is enough.

Hey, get over it!
Hope is against hope; see the reality that knocks at your door.
A life time has gone, and there you are still standing in the rear.
Take baby's steps crawl if necessary; but close the door.

Paula

Paula, there you are, strong as ever.
The pack leader, you are the Chief among the Braves.
You are the one to issue orders.
The gang will receive and proceed with your instructions.

Paula, there you are, strong as ever.
She is the nonsense stepper, waiting to straighten out the curves.
Let there not be a dot on the line, far or near, you will clear it.
The road has been paced and laced with your footsteps.

Paula, there you are, strong as ever.
You must be Jesus' Disciple on this earth.
Your character models only the tree of light.
The crick curves of man wave not with you.

Paula, there you are, strong as ever.
When the weak break, you move to hold the line of strength.
You, a straight talker, there is not any fiddling or peddling.
You beat your own drum with a deep rhyme of self-assurance.

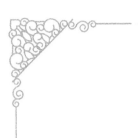

THE FORCE

An Act of Evil

Let evil dance away from me while goodness takes over my heart.
You come to me with hate in your heart and expect the same.
You call me names and expect me to strike back.
I control not my thoughts; God takes over
my tongue and even surprises me.

Let evil dance away from me while goodness takes over my heart.
Unexpectedly you warble into my lane and
place your thorns into my road.
Without control thoughts, God's words
are echoed, Lord have mercy.
The element of the Lord's Prayer begins to sing from my lips.

Let evil dance away from me while goodness takes over my heart.
I plunder as I say to myself, "Lord you are
truly in control of my thoughts."
It is through you, I sing my praises, without
a plan, your thoughts flow freely.
You are ingrained in me when evil comes upon
me, your words flow from my lips.

Let evil dance away from me while goodness takes over my heart.
Through you the world is clearer; I am
able to see beyond the moment.
It is not the present that echoes with me, it is
the ability to see beyond an evil act.
You have given me wisdom to sing your
praises, and that I am thankful.

I Too Cry

I too cry while the pain shift gears.
One day up, two days down.
It was a weary night with unbearable dreams.

I too cry while the pain shift gears.
Street names bare no shame when it comes to respect.
There is no place to lay this weary head,
survival demands strength.
Where is the sanity in this madness?

I too cry while the pain shift gears.
Glorified, my services have been rendered.
The crooked smile curved "service completed," it read.
Non-existent fantasies here just have broken dreams.

I too cry while the pain shift gears.
Threaten not your existence here, survival
generations rest upon those shoulders.
Let not today's ugliness transform into tomorrow's tragedy.
Race, legacy, strength and beauty survive through you.

Heart

Your heart is a closed up room.
Open it and let the bars flow bare.
Open it and let it believe it can live.
Open it and let it be free.

Open it and let the blemish fly free.
Open it and let the powerful waves touch
to raise the bottom that flows low.
Open it and let the broom sweep away the hurt.
Open it and let the dirt be no more.

Open it and let the waterfall flow to see the beauty it surrounds.
Open it and let the ground pound until
you see earthly worms surface.
Open it and let the skin pin up run free.
Open it and let the door bare no bars.

Open it and let and it go, so freedom can be.
Open it and let the mass on the glass form clear.
Open it and let the lily come in the spring.
Open it and let the spring bring new life.

Brown Eyed Girl

Brown eyed girl, too many responsibilities
lay upon your shoulders.

Brown eyed girl, too many times your
protector had eyed the other.

Brown eyed girl, too many times a child
reaches for the absent parent.

Brown eyed girl, too many times coffins
overflow with tomorrow's youth.

Brown eyed girl, too many times school left behind,
the street corner has become the education.

Brown eyed girl, still stand, the family
needs your survival and strength.

Interpretation

Where were you, when I stood innocently on your steps?
If there is arrogance about me, it's because I am who I am.
I know the woman in me needs not your echo.
I know my strength waits not for your approval.

I know lack of your self-worth defines me as useless.
I know your desired approval from others determine your steps.
I know your voice reach for power in others.
I know the loudness of the crowd has your consciousness.

I know the force that carries my steps, has its own drummer.
I know that drummer seizes the voice it hears.
I know when the wind comes I must act.
I know that voice that cries it must be heard.

I know your steps must feel the power.
I know you cannot stand free of the thunder.
I know your mind must be in the puzzle that rambles.
I know the rain is your rainbow, but somewhere we must bridge.

Venom

Yes, there is venom in me that has taken control.
It ripples my body tearing at the soul.
It has overtaken respect once held for authority.
Doubting Thomas is the rule that stands like the mule.

Yes, is here is venom in me that has taken control.
It can be punched with the protected symbol that cannot be erased.
It's supported with a line structure of untruth.
An airhead caught in a ruthless act.

Yes, there is venom in me that has taken control.
What will replace a rippled mind torn apart bit by pieces?
A body repaired can only truly function with a fine mind.
A true mind can touch the world without fine wine.

Yes, there is venom in me that has taken control.
The beating of the shoe still pounds on my flesh.
The word Nigger still rings in my ear; the
glob of spit rains still on my face.
Yes, there is venom in me that has taken control.

Truth

It's your truth, swallowed with dishonesty
With a smile on your face, you are viperous dangerous snake.
Six plus, model style, pressed and dressed, you are in line.
Meet and greet, stationary control, mile
line straight, your smile boxed.

It's your truth, swallowed with dishonesty.
It's a lame game, stamped carries your name.
Your patrol, you are in control.
It's your portion without a notion to end.

It's your truth, swallowed with dishonesty.
Fake out, it's a make, approved stamp, you have a deceitful smile.
A smile that will choke before it runs the tenth of a mile.
Take the poker, poke my eyes, still I stand, I do.

It's your truth, swallowed with dishonesty.
Glitter smile, bounces bitter on others, you have it all.
It's your created game, it will resolve itself.
In time, your game of ice will melt into running water.

Weight

Your system is on overload, waiting to explode.
Neglect has created this status.
Your weight will not dawn a coke-o-cola bottle.
The pounds you eat have come together to create their own home.

Your system is on overload, waiting to explode.
Pressure pushed up.
Sugar canes planted to display growth lanes.
Your frame displays a square box.

Your system is on overload, waiting to explode.
Your body movement becomes a night crawl.
Canes, rails, banister are aids to walk freely.
You are dawning upon life without quality.

Your system is on overload, waiting to explode.
Your line is not fine because your health is not of line.
Your caterpillar moves will not become a pipeline of health.
Step up, take control and let your goal be your health.

Ugly

Ugly is a conception that lies only in one's mind.
Two children looked at the same objects, processed it differently.
A child skipped happily along with new shoes.
Another child yelled, "What ugly shoes", the first child eyes tear.

Ugly is a conception that lies only in one's mind.
A face broken with years set a story,
One man of same age declared a lady unworthy of his companion.
The history that details her beauty cannot be enough by another.

Ugly is a conception lies only in one's mind.
Large structure bones displayed on one may be perceived as ugly.
The family sometimes is unable to reconnect
with loves ones to display life's beauty.
Until one day, body self-disconnects with the beauty of life.

Ugly is a conception lies only in one's mind.
Two societies, two cultures, both display images of beauty.
One society's eyes open to pin the winner as bone thin.
In another society, the person with hips is viewed with beauty.

Cocoon

Are you located in the world of the cocoon?
One that goes deep, without doors, where are you?
Are you in search of a boundary, one who looks for self?
Are you in un-rooted surface, unable to define self?

Are you located in the world of the cocoon?
Are you unable to cope and afraid to move?
Will each step you take deny you a forward move?
Are you self-boxed to stagnate your growth?

Are you located in the world of the cocoon?
Are your elements of safety cap star guarded?
Do you have a wondering soul that never stops?
Are you the risk taker that denies all boundaries?

Are you located in the world of the cocoon?
Do you have that unsettled brain?
Is it a brain that rains in your head nonstop?
A brain that is dry and cannot cry will soon go.

The Will

Death came and it wasn't so bad, only the will to live.

Family stood-by holding hands as each
breath drained from the body.

The power to control the breathing had
drained away, but not the will.

Glittering stars filled the room.

The mind slipped into deep consciousness.

Sibling touched as to console life.

The road traveled, gravel would no longer dust those feet.

The touch of strangers now encircled the lifeless body.

The peace of life serenity had come at last, beyond man's control.

Sacrifice

Black pushed back.
Livers of bodies floated in the rivers.
Three necks swung on the tree.
Another eye has opened.

The womb sprang tender feet.
The race pace sought time, the future was primed.
Dead man pleads, awaken the unborn.
Another eye had opened.

The yard swallowed his blood, a people's angel taken.
Crying seized the room, a warrior gone, another eye has opened.
Who will take his place?
Grasped and clutched strength snatched away the tears.

Blood flowed rapidly into a flood.
Freedom bell tolled.
Another eye has opened…
Tender feet moved swiftly into ones of giants.

Temporary Insanity

Temporary insanity had established her state of reality.
Alone she stood without a guard or a protector.
Yet she stood within the circle of a crowd.
What role will she play now?

Temporary insanity had established her state of reality.
Selfishness was on the bottom of her feet walk.
She walked out and went with the sprinkling lights,
But, that road refused to contain her dancing feet.

Temporary insanity had established her state of reality.
Thousand eyes lack an octopus feasted upon her image.
Her mind in search for stabilization couldn't
or wouldn't choose the right road.
She was like a goldfish in the middle of the ocean.

Temporary insanity had established her state of reality.
Companionship and intimacy were not carved.
Madness was in the midst without a solid mind in sight.
Night disappeared and day came without light.

VI

Existing

The Cobra

Cobra words capture attention; the mouth tongue is brass.
She elevates and destroys, drum's setter, stone marker, community's
pawnbroker, connects and bridges bourgeois and peasants.
The tone begins when she enters.
The prior calmness then only can truly be understood.

Cobra words capture attention; the mouth's tongue is brass.
Awesomely she stands with mouth twisted slightly.
The audience waits, digesting each word to come.
Each word will peel itself inside you.

Cobra words capture attention; the mouth's tongue is brass.
Memory will be impacted and wall framed.
Isolation matters not, the circular words
will reach beyond the beach.
Power echoes, charisma ceases, the community
to roar upon needy hour.

Cobra words capture attention; the mouth's tongue is brass.
Community needs not cry, the cobra echoes it needs.
Power motion constantly moving,
community revitalization is needy.
Today's strength transcends tomorrow's youth self-worth.

Cobra words capture attention; the mouth's tongue is brass.
The bell rings as each word stings.
Strength can and will power the hour.
Who will stand head to head with the cobra?

Cobra words capture attention; the mouth's tongue is brass.
Who will the cobra carve today?
The community's cobra bite is deadly.
Cobra swallows faces that anchor the community.

Passion

Passion is energy surged forward with great excitement.
It has strength surrounded with great
desire with love lacking at times.
Love and respect are absent when passion eyes are narrowed.
The vitality of it all cries for the itch desire to be nourished.

Passion is energy surged forward with great excitement.
It possesses only the desire to be rested and
cupped into a control of easiness.
There is a physical thrush of enthusiasm
racing to be clamped for closure.
It is a closure of passion, not love; the mind
is absent, only the body yearns.

Passion is energy surged forward with great excitement.
It is the power of the body that cries for you,
not this mind, perhaps another.
I recognize you as someone determined to
gather my thoughts into yours.
But, I cannot extend what I do have, the thought of love upon you.

Passion is energy surged forward with great excitement.
Your emotions are without a shield of protection
when mutual love stands not.
One aches passion while another seeks the true form of love.
Love is a deep drawn psycho while passion is
nothing more than a body release.

Newness

I don't know where this newness comes within me.

It is a sign of completeness that I cannot explain.

It is a peace that is set within.

It is a walk that stands on its own.

It is elevated words that need not an elevator.

Richness I observed, not in customary
eyesight, but the field flourished.

It is undeveloped richness that holds
the growth of progressiveness.

It's dominated, waking up, and breathing
air for the very first time.
It is a birth of new life, breaking out of the
womb with the senses wide open.

It is like hibernating all winter and breaking
loose into the spring air.

Africa, you claimed a lost soul that did not
know it was lost in the wilderness.

Everyday a new light bursts open, the journey continues.

Passing

Every phase is just a temporary stage for the next.

The new is a passing phase for the old.

Memories are edged into stones to give new birth.

Every day the new comes to carve tomorrow's stone.

The Helper

What will make you bite like a tick?
You pick the worse, and give them your best.
You give companionship, which the human race needs deeply.
You reach to console, when the door seemly leads nowhere.

What makes you bite like a tick?
You bring the sun when tears run.
You lift sad face when the feet just want to pace.
You seek to bind, when the wind blows separately.

What makes you bite like a tick?
You acknowledge and respect the world of
others without condemnation.
You seek to relieve pain in others.
Your vulnerability appears through others,
which make you connect.

What makes you bite like a tick?
Could it be your past that you wish not to create for a lifetime?
Could it be those ingredients you peddle for a better society?
Could it be the water that you drink not;
what will make you bite like a tick?

Respect

To respect you is to know your culture.
To know your culture is to know you.
To understand you is to love you.
You are your lifestyle.

Your life is quite simply.
You ask nothing or anyone except respect.
Respect is molded in your behavior.
You crown others with your love.

You are family connected.
The family bond that you hold binds you to your inner self.
You are one of ease, or a breath of fresh air.
You are the waves brushing ashore that grip the sand peddles.

You are the voice that echoes in the night when help is dawning.
You respond to those in need and ask nothing in return.
You appreciate value and worth in others.
Your privacy is granted because you interfere with none.

Ancestors' Legacy

Let us meet and greet through the path of our ancestors.
Let their string of hope reign within us.
When we trod, let it be with their wisdom and understanding.
Let their truth be grounded in our faith.

Let their wisdom surround us with the love of a dove.
Let their exemplary lives fill us with pride.
Let their lives be a torch to light our path.
Let the unborn generations come forth with their path.

Our present begins with the legacy of our ancestors.
Let us trod on the values they have laid before us.
Unwoven in silence, they have challenged us to move forward.
Let us acknowledge their presence as we reach into the future.

Let their faith guide us through stormy weather.
Let their lives ring anew on stony roads.
Let their love bind us together as we touch anew.
Let us greet and meet each new day with a stone from the past.

Moved

The beauty was in your soul.
You saw society partially through your parents' eyes.
Social issues ripped into society consciousness with the pen stroke.
You allowed your pen stroke to heal hunger
so others could have a meal.

The beauty was in your soul.
A hill wouldn't fill the joy you brought to your parents.
You walked and talked the song of many.
The drum beats through you for those you represented.

The beauty was in your soul.
Your legacy drummed the beat for life.
Your knife helped peel the ruins away that swallowed others.
You guided and modeled today's youth well.

The beauty was in your soul.
You left your song in the wind to carry.
We hear your words from the whistles of the wind.
We know you are near.

Survival Mold

The survival mold, it is the pen.
It will set you free.
The pen changes, control it, mold it, sanction it and personalize it.
Untangle the thoughts that crave your survival.

Things will bounce upon you that can steal your soul.
Can you find a way out without a pout?
You can find your survival mold.
Take the pen and let it destroy those demons.

The survival mold, it is the pen.
It dances with your soul when tears have covered rivers.
It opens the door to the soul when tears have covered rivers.
It melts the tears away when the face needs a glimpse of fresh air.

The survival mold, it is the pen.
It creates a safe world when everything else has been taken away.
It holds memories that can only be explored through the pen.
It is sanity that is needed for survival

Making It

You can achieve against all odds if the confidence lies within you.
Your potential is within your hands if you grasp all avenues.
When people bag you out, take it, wear it, and achieve over it.
Let others see your smile when tears ache beneath your eyes.

You can achieve against all odds if the confidence lies within you.
Take a moment to project a successful dream that should come;
When they had stuck pens in torn clothes
it was just to see your blood.
Let each day open with a dream that shall
shield you from the madness.

You can achieve against all odd if the confidence lies within you.
When they call you names, rise above their game of insecurity.
It is their inhumanity that's deep rooted lies within their minds.
Let them not take you into their dungeon.

You can achieve against all odd if the confidence lies within you.
They see you and they are unable to free them from your spirit.
You are a gifted spirit; they will dance a life time in caged minds.
Sticks and stones will always be in your
path, but you must not succumb.

Purity

God knows the pureness of all, nothing else matters.
When the final curtain calls, he will be the only judge.
When honest mistakes are made, its baby learned knowledge.
Many times the learner sits and watches
without a knowledgeable ego.

God knows the pureness of all, nothing else matters.
Man's words flow constantly, bound with truth and falsehood.
But, God is the only sifter; through him
we stand straight or curved.
Many times the book that opens easily,
have rigs that are never read.

God knows the pureness of all, nothing else matters.
Words are words, actions are greater, and that is true.
It is the humble child who comes in God's greatness.
When the heart is pure, the maimed will stand with God's greatest.

God's knows the pureness of all, nothing else matters.
Hearts are cleared when three trail lines have been walked.
The walls and halls are opened when
truth is set forth with honesty.
God has great compassion with those who exalts the truth.

God knows the pureness of all, nothing else matters.
When hearts are opened, God's patience will reign.
It is through God we seek everlasting life, the gift of salvation.
The bare soul is open to God and others who have eyes to see.

God knows the pureness of all, nothing else matters.
Roads will always be open to those who seek an honest look.
Falsehood is not God's way; neither should it be man.
Man is perfect not, but this should not be used
as an excuse, to cover up his faults.

God knows the pureness of all, nothing else matters.
The true fruit will always blossom to give new birth.
The fullness of God's prayers will be received in God's kingdom.
While empty prayers will be received as bottomless buckets.

Retirement

Society rings it bell; you have
served the community well.

Your impact has laid a direct path
for youth to carve their stone.

Retirement has not secluded you from
carving another stone in society.

Your quality life has opened up ways for
youth to create their own path.

You have retreated not from life.

You have just chosen to meditate
on the element of life before you.

You have laid the road for few.

Those few have modeled your method into thousands.

The love you give has transcended into other lives.

When they see you, they lace their faces with smiles.

Your story is relived each day with those you embraced.

Your touch continues to inspire and enrich lives.

It is the human touch you gave that has
been implanted in youth.

This human touch reaches generations,
yet unborn, for human justice.

Your retirement has not stopped
the ideas you implanted in others.

Unlock Your Door

Stop, wait, and receive, the path is open.
Morning will come; you can then pen the cloth.
Perceive the direction first to step forward.
There will be a glare on top edged in stone.

Stop, wait, and receive, the path is open.
There will be many roads calling you.
Be not eager to catch those that rush forward,
the wise man waits to receive.
The toad that stumbles last may hold the key, you search.

Stop, wait, and receive, the path is open.
The first door lies not always with the answer.
In the silence of night, the right answer may be thrust upon you.
Horns and sirens may come forth with
fluttering answers in all directions.

Stop, wait, and receive, the path is open.
The correct path, waits inching from your feet, perhaps.
When you are there, the pen will glow and you will know.
Stop, wait, and receive, the path is right there, before you.

Stumbling Forward

Batter me, devastate me, but let me have
the wisdom to move away.
Let me sing into the ring of hope.
Let me walk with strong legs to carry my own.
Let me move with a swift step, not to
tarry on yesterday's weakness.

Batter me, devastate me, but let me have
the wisdom to move away.
Let me move with a band to carry a warm tune.
Let me walk in life to strengthen those that are weak.
Let me create to move forward without hindering others.

Batter me, devastate me, but let me have
the wisdom to move away.
Let me come into life to seal and highlight those on a higher plane.
Let me free myself of those who lives are centered on negativism.
Let me see the path that lead and provide directions.

Batter me, devastate me, but let me have
the wisdom to move away.
Let strength come to those who marvelously move forward.
Let there be an atmosphere conducive to
spring forward to open doors.
Let us march forward to unlatch byways that are stumbling blocks.

Stand or Not

Where do you stand?
The gang has frowned upon those who have taken the lesser road.
Where do you stand?
Can you stand away from the crowd to play your own tune?

Where do you stand?
Are you capable of singing your own song without a back up band?
Where do you stand?
Can you free yourself from the magnet of others?

Where do you stand?
What is your ulterior motives if you stand as self?
Where do you stand?
Can you stand among many to beat a different drum?

Where do you stand?
Is it when rows are neatly lined in order
with their own string quartet?
Can you step to a new drummer to create your own band?
Where do you stand?

Where do you stand?
Just tell me this day.
The crowd is pulling you one way.
But, your eyes are focused on the lesser
traveled road that lies before you.

Tell me this day.
Where do you stand?

"Flavia"

Where have you taken the flavor?
Will it be the flavor that has pleased all crabs in a basket?
Will it be the one that has smoothed the
boat over the stormy water?
Will it be the one that hold the elements of peace for the mind?

Where have you taken the flavor?
It is the quietness of the drum beat that
summons the crowd I need.
It is the call of the tone that can tame the wild wolf.
It is the aroma that comes with a restful smell.

Where have you taken the flavor?
It is the flavor tone that stands in the uniqueness among thousands.
It is the flavor that separates you when trouble creeps into cracks.
It is the one free of side, one that seeks to bind and compromise.

Where have you taken the flavor?
It is the flavor that sets me on a straight path with free thoughts.
It is the flavor that comes with un-bridged love for all men.
It is a smile to receive and one that condemns not.

False Hope

What is this claim that has overridden your emotions?
You have been given a promotion to move
out of the picture, now go!
What is your obsession on another human being?
Is it a lack of self-esteem, trying to prove one-self through another?

Has your self-doubt led you to this state?
What is it, the lack of directions you have received in life?
Is it the cry of you trying to be whole at another's expense?
Is it your self-doubt that you are constantly
replaying through others?

Is it your inability to accept the reality of your rejection?
Is it your false perception of self that kneel
and seek another approval?
What is it, your insecurity that has doors open all around you?
What is it, an obsessed desire that has
taken control over your mind?

What is this fixation you have over another human being?
You refuse to let go, a mind reads adjustment is deeply needed.
A clear line has been drawn; you are completely out of the picture.
It is past yonder time to reconstruct your life and move forward.

The Blind Road

The dangling coins are outdated.
The machine now has flinching lights.
A man begins to express joy like a boy.
The heart starts to beat.

The dangling coins are outdated.
The paper carries the weight.
A billion or trillion is not enough for the habit.
Yet, a penny is a bit too much for the feed.

The dangling coins are outdated.
A new world has claimed the mind.
It is in a total bind, out of control.
Without a bit of a bite, waiting and lingering for a hit.

The dangling coins are outdated.
The mortgage, the insurance and the taxes need to be paid.
It is a dance lace that will soon come to a climax.
Who will win this constant merry-go-round?

The dangling coins are outdated.
The phone rings without a pick up.
It is a pillow bounce about without a cushion.
It calls and malls on a hopeless mind.

The dangling coins are outdated.
One step forward, ten backward.
It is an unfair game of give and take.
It is the name game of gambling.

Rejuvenation

It is the vigor of the community we seek.
The dogs will bark when they hear an unfamiliar sound.
The children will again jump rope in the street with huge smiles.
The birds will flutter the community songs.

It is the vigor of the community we seek.
The cats will meow and cuddle on the couch wiggling its tail.
The street cleaner will deposit trash that has lingered on the street.
The park will be filled with barbecues,
family gatherings and laughter.

It is the vigor of the community we seek.
It is the livelihood of the community we seek to bring forth.
It is the warmth of the elders sharing stories on the park benches.
It is the school band marching their stuff
proudly for the public to see.

It is the vigor of the community we seek.
We seek to rebuild and renew the elements in the community.
We seek freedom and newness in the
community through ourselves.
Through us, we gather freedom to renew and rebuild.

Changes

Step ladder changes are here.
They are descending upward and downward.
Whooping changes, wallop and deep, all mixed in the same bowl.
Mini steps getting lost, leaving one step
hanging on the ladder, unstable.

Deep step ladder changes.
There aren't meals to deal with this hunger.
Gallop steps causes me to fall, forces me to regroup.
Where is the glove to catch the hit just bounced off my head?

Step ladder changes crying out to be saved here.
Where is the recognition of that dream that never was real?
Reality based upon falsehood, only to find
out after a whole life has escaped.
Baby steps, baby steps, galloped into one
giant leap over night, an awaking.

Step ladder changes crying out.
An awaking, with little space to move
forward in an unbridged field
A mind reaping in truth, with baby's steps.
Dreams gone, with a mind haven been deep rooted in falsehood.

Ollie Marshall is a native of Springfield, Arkansas, from the community of Union Chapel, where she grew up with ten brothers and five sisters. She now makes her home in Orange, New Jersey, with her husband. She is a retired teacher from Newark Public School System. She speaks through her poetry.

Changes are within me, bridge leaping, outward, under and over.
Scattered nerves are rocking within me.
Sometimes they are creepy crawls.
Nerves are crawling inch by inch throughout this body itching.
Happiness, sadness, joy, boldness, serene, these cries are all within me.
Whooping changes, wallop and deep, all mixed in the same bowl.
Mini steps getting lost, leaving one step hanging on the
ladder, unstable meeting the sane...life in the raw.

Ollie has published five other books: The ABC Character Builder, Fire In My Bones, Commander In Chief (The 44th President), Searching- Genealogy-Connecting-Phase 1, Sprouts of the Spirit.

Printed in the USA
CPSIA information can be obtained
at www.ICGtesting.com
LVHW052109220624
783667LV00009B/513